Traction Engines in Review

Traction Engines

in Review

by Barry J. Finch AIIP
with text by Jack Hampshire

 LONDON

First published 1971

SBN 7110 0234 7

Published by Ian Allan Ltd, Shepperton, Surrey, and printed in the
United Kingdom by Balding + Mansell Ltd, London and Wisbech

Contents

Acknowledgements

Most of the pictures I have of Traction Engines have been obtained with the co-operation of their owners and drivers. I would like to say thank you to all those who have given this co-operation so willingly to enable me to obtain the pictures reproduced in this book.

I would also like to acknowledge the help so readily given by Mr A. Duke, Mr E. A. Fillmore, Mr C. G. Mileham and Mr K. M. Vigus who have been of great assistance in the production of the captions.

Finally I would like to say how interesting and entertaining I found the words of Mr J. Hampshire and hope that with the pictures they will prove to be of interest to all who have a love of steam engines.

Barry J. Finch

The National Traction Engine Club covers all aspects of the Traction Engine hobby. For details write to the secretary Geo. F. Beck, 127, Greensted Road, Loughton, Essex.

Introduction

Many thousands of words have been written in the last decade describing the merits of the various makes, models and breeds of traction engines, road rollers, tractors, agricultural engines, ploughing engines, road locomotives, steam wagons and the lowly portable engine, so that it becomes increasingly difficult for the fellow who only worked with steam engines all his life to find something new to write about. The mind virtually boggles at what has been written about their working parts, vital statistics, the chaps who designed them and the works where they were built, to say nothing of the men who found glory in the manufacture of these, to me, majestic machines.

For my part, as Brer Rabbit said, "I was born and bred in the briar patch" of steam engines. Fortunately or otherwise, according to how you view it, I was bitten by a "steam bug" at a very early age, and have suffered from "steam fever" ever since. I have been told, and there seems no earthly reason to disprove it, that I was weaned on hot oil, steam and coal dust, in which case you have the logical reason for my extraordinary behaviour when near to a steam engine or even discussing one. So when Barry Finch,

a friend of some years standing, asked me to write something about traction engines for his book of photographs my mind went floating off and away on a beautiful cloud of nostalgic memories. Not to the days of my youth spent in learning what made a steam engine "tick", but to the time when I, and the many men I knew, drove them along the highway for a living fifty and more years ago. Those were the days when you had to have steam in your engine and be out of the yard by 6am, and thought yourself extremely lucky if you were back again ten to twelve hours later. Yet at the end of the week you felt like a millionaire with 25s in your pocket as wages.

I have often asked myself why I ever drove a steam engine when I could have had a far easier job, for my hands, face and clothing were perpetually black and I was so tired at the end of the day that, more often than not, I nearly fell out of the tender. Yet for some inexplicable reason, many years later I find myself still talking and writing about—and given the chance, playing with—steam engines. I wonder why?

Fishbourne, Isle of Wight

Jack Hampshire

1 Portable Engines

The steam "Portable Engine" was indeed a wonderful machine for general-purpose work in the early days of steam power. It was used to very good account on large estates, by farmers and contractors, for sawmilling, threshing and a thousand and one different jobs long before the turn of the century. Although by 1910 they were fast falling out of favour I can recall a number in regular use after 1920, and as late maybe as 1930 there were still a few working, but more in a specific job as stationary power in sawmills. I remember a small 2nhp (nominal horse power) Garrett portable working quite happily on a farm in Sussex in 1940 doing the ordinary daily chores of chaff cutting, corn crushing and milling. On the other side of the scale as recently as 1960 a 12nhp portable was still in action in a sawmill in the Isle of Wight, but there must surely now be very few survivors.

Portable engines were available in a great variety of powers; 5 to 10nhp for general-purpose work, but they were obtainable in much higher or lower ratings according to requirements. As an apprentice I helped in the repair of one of 30nhp doing duty in a large brickyard, driving brick and pipe-making machinery. Quite a number were specially built by Marshall's of Gainsborough to the order of the Home Grown Timber Commission in 1940. These were 10 to 15nhp double cylinder types to be used for sawmill work in various parts of the country during the war.

The word "portable", of course, merely denoted that the engine was mounted on four wheels, thus enabling it to be towed, usually by a team of horses, from job to job. A truly magnificent sight in those far off days was a team of four, five, or even six beautiful shire horses pulling a portable engine along the untarred roads.

I was once shown an instruction book issued by Fowler's round about 1890. In it I remember reading; . . . "As a driver you will be expected to wear a peaked cap or a bowler hat on duty to denote your rank, for you are now in a position above that of a labourer." Somehow I cannot reconcile this to the portable engine driver. My experience of him was that his job seemed not to call for any high degree of skill from an engineering point of view. Many incidents, some humorous, some fatal, were caused by such lack of knowledge. This brings to mind a chap who drove a portable in East Sussex. A bigger beer swiller and poacher would be hard to find, and his ignorance as an engineer was surpassed only by his drinking ability. He once had occasion to repair the governor belt, and through lack of "know-how" made a poor job of it, which sparked off the following train of events. After a brief spell of work the belt repair parted allowing the governors to stop and the engine to race out of control. The vibration thus caused brought the uncared for, tall chimney crashing down, a part of which hit the safety valve sufficiently hard to dislodge it from its seating. The roar of escaping steam so startled the poor old horse which stood half asleep harnessed to the water-cart that it straightway bolted. In its flight it ran over the old fellow and crushed his leg, so ending his career as a driver. Such were the tribulations endured by horses and portable engine drivers of yesteryear.

Clayton & Shuttleworth Portable "*Nellie*". 5nhp.
Single cylinder/SV. Photographed at Ross-on-Wye.

(*Above*) Marshall Portable No 87866. Single cylinder/PV. Type S. Fitted with Britannia-type boiler and circular firebox.

(*Left*) Ransomes, Sims & Jefferies Portable No 27268 "*Little Lucy*". Built 1917. 4nhp. Single cylinder/SV.

(*Right*) Davey Paxman Portable No 11692. Built 1900. Single cylinder/SV.

(*Far right*) Humphries Portable No 1663. Single cylinder/SV.

(*Above*) Marshall Portable. Type S. Single cylinder/PV.
(*Far left*) Foster Portable No 14737. Built 1942. 8nhp.
Single cylinder/SV. Photographed at Revesby.
(*Left*) Ruston & Hornsby Portable. Built 1921. 4nhp.
Photographed at Pickering.
(*Right*) Ruston & Hornsby Portable No 8623. Built 1903.
Single cylinder/SV.

Ransomes, Sims & Jefferies Portable No 14704.
Built 1903. 6nhp. Single cylinder/SV.

Farmers Foundry Portable No 36. Built 1910. 7nhp.
DCC/SV.

Farmers Foundry Portable No 39. Built 1912. 6nhp. DCC/SV. This engine is the last one built by Farmers Foundry.

Ruston Portable No 163853. Single cylinder/PV. Class 320. Mark J.

(*Above*) Garrett Portable. Type WSII. Single
cylinder/PV.
(*Right*) Clayton & Shuttleworth Portable No 34986.
Built 1902. Single cylinder/SV.

2 *The Agricultural Traction Engine*

The start of it all, I suppose, was when Richard Trevithick first made a steam engine to travel along the road under its own power at Camborne, in Cornwall. As the years passed experiments were made by scores of other engineers and with the passage of time the steam traction engine was evolved. Gradually the poor old horse was dispensed with for general farm work, especially from his duties of driving farm machinery, such as corn-mills, small threshing machines and other plant by means of what was known as the "horse gear".

Slowly but surely the agricultural traction engine grew in popularity with farmers, estate owners and contractors alike, so that by the 1890s it had, except for the odd occasion, almost ousted the portable steam engine. By then literally dozens of engineering firms were jumping on the wagon, as it were, vying with each other to produce the best machine, each claiming his engine to be more powerful, economical and foolproof than any other. All sorts of contrivances were brought to bear by the various makers to achieve this end. The main advance in economy was the discovery of the vast amount of expansion to high-pressure steam, thus making possible the compounding of cylinders. In other words, as the steam was exhausted from one cylinder (the high pressure), it was led to another (the low pressure), and so used a second time by continued expansion before being discharged up the chimney into the atmosphere, thereby effecting a great saving in both fuel and water.

In the quest for greater economy many different types of valve gear were tried with varying degrees of success. Hackworth, Joy and Stevenson were the three most well known; Stevenson unquestionably taking pride of place with most traction engine manufacturers. Although Stevenson's gear required two eccentrics to operate the valve for each cylinder, Joy's method needed only one, but the wear in the many joints and pins soon outweighed its gain over the two-eccentric system, leaving Stevenson's gear as the master for portables, traction engines, locomotives and steam wagons alike, with the odd exception of course. It is only fair to add that all valve gears had their good points, depending largely upon the type of steam engine on which it was employed.

The ways and means of increasing the heating surface by the number and size of fire-tubes also played a big part in the economy. So too did the various fireboxes such as the Garrett patent corrugated top firebox, Marshall's patent firebox, and the round firebox of Robey's.

What with Wallis & Steevens' patent "Expansion Gear", dozens of different makes of mechanical lubricator, British and American patented injectors, White's water lifter, So-and-so's boiler fluid, Pickering governors and Klinger safety water gauge glasses, I'm beginning to wonder whether old Zed Foster was after all so far from the truth when he referred to traction engines, quite seriously, as "They o' traption ingins".

I have often been asked the question, "Where does the agricultural engine finish and the road locomotive begin?" This is a little difficult to define, but it is usually taken as read that the agricultural traction engines could be recognised by the following points: they were mostly unsprung at the front and rear axles, and were practically all of the single-cylinder type, although the compound engine was not unknown. The "Burrell" single-crank compound was an outstanding example of this. Most manufacturers fitted their engines with boiler-feed pump only; injectors were supplied as a special order. All were built with roping drums and 75 yards of wire rope, band brake to work either the back axle or the intermediate shaft, their own governors, or Pickering's, to order, two-speed gears, and tender tank only. Their weights ranged from 9 to 15 tons, with nominal horse powers of from 5 to 8. The hind wheels were iron shod and drilled to take "spuds" or "paddles" for use on soft ground. They had a legal speed limit of 4mph and were by law entitled to pull a train of three wagons of not more than four wheels each and a water cart.

Foolproofing of engines was spoken of in an earlier paragraph. This is not so fantastic as it may at first appear, for in the hands of an unintelligent driver a boiler can become a high-powered bomb. Many boiler explosions occurred during the period between 1850 and 1900 either through lack of knowledge or bravado on the part of the drivers. It was quite common for them to screw down the "Salter" safety valve to obtain a higher pressure just to prove that the engine was more powerful than that of their rivals. Again, if an engine was bogged down the driver would, more often than not, apply this desperate method of gaining extra pressure to make the machine pull itself out of the mire, instead of employing the orthodox use of jacks and timber. Many drivers have lost their lives and the owners their engines through this most dangerous practice.

At about the turn of the century boiler insurance became more readily available and with it a rigorous boiler examination by a competent engineer. This, coupled with the fitting of the Ramsbottom safety valve, and other types that could be "locked", made the "extra pressure" foolhardiness virtually impossible, thereby reducing the explosion risk to that of those caused by purely accidental reasons.

I have no desire to dwell upon the awful havoc an explosion can cause, but I remember only too clearly as a very young boy being taken to see the result of one of these a few days after it had happened, and the impact remains vividly with me to this day. It occurred at the home farm of a big estate on the Surrey/Sussex border. According to the facts gleaned at the time of our visit it seems that the top motion of an old Hornsby traction engine had been removed and the boiler was in use to supply steam to a 4nhp vertical steam engine used for driving the corngrinder and other equipment. During the lunch hour it was the practice of the farm hands to use the engine house as a dining room in cold weather. On such an occasion as this a few of the farm hands were in the engine house eating their meal when, without any warning, the butt-joint gave way on the underside of the boiler shell and split wide open. The noise and roar must have been shattering. When I saw it the boiler had been blown completely upside down and lay some five or six yards from where it had been housed. The roof of the building had been blown away together with one of the brick walls, and with it all went the lives of three men.

(*Left*) Allchin Traction Engine No 1652.
Registration No EB 4938. Built 1914. 6nhp.
(*Below*) Aveling & Porter Traction Engine
No 9096. Registration No AF 6001. Built 1920.
6nhp.

(*Above*) Burrell Traction Engine No 2767.
Registration No YA 1683. Built 1905. 6nhp.
9 tons. SCC.
(*Left*) Burrell Traction Engine No 3586.
"*Warrior*". Registration No BP 5921.
Built 1914. 7nhp. 12½ tons. SCC.

(*Top left*) Burrell Traction Engine No 4049 "*Daphne*".
Registration No TW 5228. Built 1926. 6nhp.
(*Left*) Burrell Traction Engine "*Millenium King*".
Registration No EB 8351. SCC.

Clayton & Shuttleworth Traction Engine No 46823.
"*Dusty*". Registration No KE 4173. Built 1914. 7nhp.
10 tons. Single cylinder. Photographed at Gillingham in
1970.

Opposite
(*Top*) Burrell Traction Engine No 4048 "*William the
Second*". Registration No PW 8905. Built 1926. 7nhp.
Single Cylinder. Photographed at Haslemere 1970.
(*Bottom*) Burrell Traction Engine No 2003 "*Diamond
Queen*". Registration No YA 509. Built 1897. 6nhp.
$8\frac{1}{2}$ tons. SCC.

(*Above*) Fowler Traction Engine No 9698.
Registration No HR 4732. Built 1903. 6nhp.
11 tons. Single cylinder. Class A4.
(*Above right*) Fowler Traction Engine No 13600
"*Challenger*". Registration No NO 1449. Built 1914.
8nhp.
(*Right*) Fowler Traction Engine No 13140.
Registration No Y 9955. Built 1913. 7nhp.
Photographed at Appleford 1970.

Opposite
Fowell Traction Engine No 108. Registration
No EW 2981. Built 1922. 8nhp. Single cylinder.

(*Above*) Garrett Traction Engine No 32936 "*Felsted Belle*". Registration No ER 603. Built 1916. 7nhp.
(*Right*) Marshall Traction Engine No 66001. Registration No OS 872. Built 1914. 7nhp. Single cylinder. Photographed at Lingfield 1970.

(*Above*) Marshall Traction Engine No 54587. "*Pride of the Road*". Registration No AJ 5781 Built 1910. 10½ tons. Single cylinder.
(*Right*) Marshall Traction Engine No 61880. Registration No FL 3942. Built 1913. 7nhp. 10 tons. Single cylinder.

(*Above*) Ruston Proctor Traction Engine No 35501 "*The Muddler*". Registration No BE 7438. Built 1908. 8nhp. 11 tons.

(*Top right*) McLaren Traction Engine No 1642. 5nhp. 2 cylinders.

(*Right*) Ransomes, Sims & Jefferies Traction Engine No 15278 "*Chieftain*". Registration No NO 2009. Built 1903. 7nhp. Single cylinder.

Opposite

Marshall Traction Engine No 84562 "*Daphne-Ann*". Registration No KP 6969. Built 1926. 6nhp. 10½ tons. Single cylinder.

Ransomes, Sims & Head Traction Engine No 5137.
Registration No Z 1. Built 1876. 4nhp. 7 tons. Single
cylinder.

Opposite
Closeups of Ransomes, Sims & Head No 5137.

(*Above*) Wallis & Steevens Traction
Engine No 7269 "*Panther*". Registration
No NO 3343. Built 1912. 7nhp. $10\frac{1}{2}$ tons.
Single cylinder.
(*Left*) Wallis & Steevens Traction Engine
No 4078 "*Goliath*". Registration No
GRX 400. Built 1902. 3nhp. 3 tons.
Single cylinder.

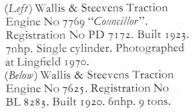

(*Left*) Wallis & Steevens Traction
Engine No 7769 "*Councillor*".
Registration No PD 7172. Built 1923.
7nhp. Single cylinder. Photographed
at Lingfield 1970.
(*Below*) Wallis & Steevens Traction
Engine No 7625. Registration No
BL 8283. Built 1920. 6nhp. 9 tons.

Wantage Traction Engine No 1522 "*Pioneer*".
Registration No BW 4415. Built 1905. 8nhp.
Photographed at Acrise 1970.

34

3 Ploughing Engines

Working our way up through the scale of agricultural engines, the next on the list would be ploughing engines. And, no greater name in the world of ploughing tackle was there than that of John Fowler & Co Ltd, of Leeds. Again I am being a little unfair by quoting one name when so many other engineers made their mark in contributions to the agricultural world. Burrell's, of Thetford, for example, built many sets of plough tackle, including the single-engine set of gear, and the "mechanical digger" attachment for traction engines. Aveling & Porter, too, of Rochester, made a great number of sets. Another great name to add to the list of producers of plough tackle was that of Mc-Laren, of Leeds, a well-known one indeed in the sphere of traction engines. Every one of these firms made wonderful engines and ploughing equipment, but somehow they just couldn't match the perfection of Fowler's. Don't ask me why this was, for although I have driven ploughing engines on many occasions to help someone out of a difficulty, I am *not* a *ploughman*. But I feel sure that all plough-engine drivers and ploughmen would agree with me that the engines and equipment made by Fowler's reached the acme of perfection in the early 1900s, holding that honour until an inglorious end was thrust upon them round about the '35/'40s.

Looking back over the years when as a youth, with my father and brother, I would visit the Smithfield Fat Stock Show at Christmas, then held at Islington; on Fowler's stand there would always be one of their latest sets, and as usual there would be the placard standing on the running board of one engine, proclaiming that it had been "SOLD to Lord ***," or "**** Esq.", followed by the name of the estate. Immaculate in their spotless new paint, they were indeed awe-inspiring with their gigantic size. They could have been a pair of BBs of 14nhp, BB1s of 16nhp, or even AA7s of 18nhp.

Fowler's did not make the 18nhp engine their maximum size, for I remember seeing two 22nhp engines dredging out wreckage, mud and stones from just offshore of the Town Quay at Southampton sometime around the 1930s. I am given to understand that they built them up to 35hp at their works in Germany, and made a few of these same dimensions in their Leeds works for the Russian Government.

When one looks at all the equipment which goes to make up a set of ploughing tackle one is first of all struck by the immensity of everything. The engines could be anything from 18 to 25 tons each in weight according to the type; the huge anti-balance plough with its two opposing sets of turn-furrows, the cultivator with its massive tynes, its lifting gear and turning device, the land press with its "V"-shaped rimmed wheels, the wide beam with the harrows attached which would cover many square yards when set up for work, the mole plough with its 4in mole, the huge water cart that would take water out to either engine upon request at the appropriate signal being given on the steam whistle, and finally the plough van wherein the crew of five or six would spend the night in well-earned rest.

From my own experience of living in the van, it could not be said to compare, even remotely, with the amenities of Claridge's or the Dorchester, but when all the crew were gathered together inside on a cold night you could at least claim to be warm. You will notice, of course, that I have omitted the word *comfortable*. With the top of the coal-fire stove glowing red, the rabbit, poached that morning, bubbling away in the pot with vegetables gleaned most likely by the same dubious means, the paraffin lamp hanging on the wall fighting for survival against tobacco smoke so thick that you could not recognise the fellow sitting opposite, except by his voice—this then is a glimpse of a ploughman's van life.

Before leaving the subject of van life, my friend Rex, a plough-engine driver of some years standing, told me of an incident when the crew, celebrating a record ploughing acreage in the local pub, imbibed a little too freely and became involved in a row with some of the local lads. At long last they staggered back to the van to sleep. Much later, Joe, the foreman, had occasion to rise from his bed and leave the van for a specific purpose. He returned seconds later with blood streaming down his face declaring in a loud voice that he had been attacked by someone. Immediately the rest of the crew tumbled out of bed to deal with Joe's assailant. In the darkness and their semi-stupor they were stalking each other. When daylight came it was discovered that Joe in his haste had trodden on the end of the ash-hoe leaning against one of the engine wheels, and the iron handle had swung out and hit him. There is a moral here somewhere if only I could find it.

A few facts and figures here might be of interest. For instance:

Deep Ploughing. Taking a pair of 18hp engines, 6 furrows at a time could be ploughed, and on light soils 7. The daily average could be 20 acres.

Scarifying. For hard ground 11 tynes were commonly used. In soft ground, wing tynes were fitted, making 13 all told. An average of 30 acres daily could be achieved.

Mole Draining. A 4in mole was used, being pulled through the ground some 27in deep to leave a hole like a drain pipe that would stay open for from 15 to 20 years. Some have been known to remain open for up to 30 years. To achieve this extremely heavy duty a double rope was used. That is, the rope from the drum on the engine passed through a snatch-block attached to the draw-bar of the mole plough, then returned to the engine and was fastened by a shackle to an eye arranged for this purpose on the hind wheel of the engine.

A pair of 18hp engines would consume from 15 to 20cwt of coal a day each, according to whether they were working on heavy duty or light and on the quality of the coal. This would include the amount required for raising steam in the morning and banking down at night.

The normal crew for a steam plough set would be five or six according to the nature of the work. This would comprise of two drivers and two ploughmen, one of whom would be the foreman. It was he who set out the work and determined the direction in which, for drainage purposes, the furrows would run. Finally there would be the cook who would also have to be capable of taking over an engine as a relief driver, and acting as a relief ploughman as and when required.

The crew of a steam plough outfit was about the best example of team work to be found. No one asked what they had to do; it came as second nature. Take scarifying as an example. Since there was probably 1,000 yards of wire rope between your engine and the other, it could be that one engine was out of sight over the brow of a hill, so you worked by signals given on the steam whistles. When it came to your turn to pull you gripped the lever to drop the dog clutch in and pulled slowly for a few yards while the cultivator lifted its tynes and turned round. The man operating that machine released the lifter catch at the right moment and the tynes dropped deep into the ground again, a fact that you were aware of because the engine slowed up. You then increased the power by opening the regulator and the rope came humming in through the coiling gear on to your rope drum. The operator on the cultivator would signal with his arms whether he wanted you to increase speed or lower it. If he were out of sight the driver of the other engine would pass the signal by appropriate whistles. You continued to pull the cultivator towards you until it was within a few yards, then gradually you decreased the speed until the shackle on the end of the rope was within a foot or so of the

Burrell Ploughing Engine No 777. Built 1879. 8nhp.
Single cylinder.

coiling gear jockey wheel before stopping the engine. If your
speed was too great at the end of the pull the momentum imparted
to the rope drum on the engine at the other end would cause a
few turns of rope to fall out of position, which meant much heavy
work, loss of time and plenty of bad language re-coiling the

sagging rope. If all was well you signalled to the other engine
driver that you were out of gear, and he would begin to pull the
cultivator towards him. When it was about 20 yards away from
you, you put your engine into low gear and moved up the width
of the cultivator ready for your next pull. You took this oppor-
tunity to top up the boiler with water via the injector, make up
your fire, and then waited for the signal to pull again. This cycle
continued until the end of the day or the end of the job.

(*Above*) Fowler Ploughing Engine No 13880.
Registration No NO 371. Built 1917. 18nhp. Class AA.
(*Right*) Fowler Ploughing Engine No 13881.
Registration No NO 372. Built 1917. 18nhp. Class AA.

Opposite
Fowler Ploughing Engines Nos 13481 and 13482.
Registration Nos NO 796 and NO 797. Built 1913.
16nhp. Class BB. Photographed at Great Bookham 1970.

(*Above*) Cultivator in use in Essex 1960.
(*Right*) Cultivator at work in Essex 1965.

(*Above*) Fowler Ploughing Engine No 14213.
Registration No FCF 126D. Built 1914. 14nhp. Class BB.
(*Right*) Fowler Ploughing Engine No 15203.
Registration No BH 7344. Built 1918. 16nhp. Class BB1.

Fowler Ploughing Engine No 15226 *"Tiny Tim"*.
Registration No NR 77. Built 1918. 16nhp. Class BB1.

Opposite
Fowler Ploughing Engine No 15363 *"Tiger"*.
Registration No NK 989. Built 1919. 18nhp. Class AA7.

(*Above*) Fowler Ploughing Engine No 2693.
Registration No NR 1212. Built 1886.
14nhp. Class AA. Single cylinder.
Photographed at Rempstone 1957.
(*Right*) Fowler Ploughing Engine No 15142.
Registration No BP 6125. Built 1918.
16nhp. Class BB1.

44

(*Above*) Fowler Ploughing Engine No 15172 "*Satan*". Registration No AC 9494. 16nhp. Class BB1.
(*Left*) Fowler Ploughing Engine No 14712 "*Wilbur*". Registration No NO 4630. Built 1917. 14nhp. Class BB.

45

(*Above*) Fowler Ploughing Engine No 14727.
Registration No NO 223. Built 1918. 18nhp.
Class AA7.
(*Right*) Fowler Ploughing Engine No 15226
"*Tiny Tim*". Registration No NR·77.
Built 1918. 16nhp. Class BB1.

(*Above*) Fowler Ploughing Engine No 13877
"*Sir John*". Registration No NO 5.
Built 1917. 18nhp. Class AA. Photographed
at Sudbury.
(*Right*) Fowler Ploughing Engine No 15182.
Registration No HO 5868. Built 1918.
Photographed at Bexleyheath.

Fowler Ploughing Engine No 1368 "*Margaret*".
Registration No AL 8468. Built 1870. 12nhp. Single
cylinder. Photographed at Cropedy 1967.

4 *Showman's and Contractors' Road Locomotives*

To my mind, man, in all his wisdom in connection with steam locomotion, reached his supreme culmination with the production of the "Road Locomotives" of the late 1920s. They were awe-inspiring to be near. Majestic in their movement, Herculean in strength, yet in the hands of a competent driver as docile as a lamb.

There were many engineering firms which played a big part in the ultimate mechanical perfection of the road locomotive. Here again I am being unfair by quoting just three of the most famous and well loved of them all; Charles Burrell & Sons, of Thetford, John Fowler & Co, of Leeds, and William Foster & Sons, of Lincoln.

The last road locomotive built under the patents of Charles Burrell & Sons, a name revered by all true lovers of steam traction, was completed by Garrett's of Leiston in 1930, works No 4092, and named *Simplicity*, to the order of A. Deakin & Sons, the well-known showman family of Brynmawr, Brecon. By some unfortunate misunderstanding, alas, long after she had left the show world she fell to the scrap merchants' oxy-acetylene torch, and every lover of the steam road locomotive mourned her passing. I believe that I am safe in saying that Charles Burrell & Sons built more contractors' and showman's road locomotives than any other maker from 1886 to 1930, the date when this well-beloved firm ceased to operate.

John Fowler & Co, of Leeds, completed the last of their showman's locomotives in 1934, works No 20223 and named *Supreme*, to the order of Mrs A. Deakin, of Brynmawr. This outstandingly elegant engine is mercifully with us still. Now beautifully restored she will, it is hoped, remain in perpetuity for all to

see and ponder upon. According to the records, John Fowler & Co catered for the showman's needs from 1886 to 1934, a truly wonderful achievement.

The third in the world of road locomotives is William Foster & Co, of Lincoln. Many beautiful and well-known contractors' and showman's engines were built by them throughout the years between 1904 until 1934. They were perhaps better known in the show world than in the contractors', but in either case they were rivals to be respected by other manufacturers. The last showman's engine produced by this firm was the 7nhp *Princess Marina*, works No 14634, for T. Drakely, of Birmingham.

Other well-known names such as Foden, McLaren, Garrett, Savage and Wallis & Steevens produced a number throughout the years, and left no mean mark in the annals of the road locomotive.

To clarify the subtle difference between Scenic, Showman and Contractor:

Scenic was of 8nhp and over. Fitted with a lifting crane on the tender for the purpose of lifting the heavy "scenic railway" cars on to the platform rails. Invariably these locomotives were fitted with a second dynamo known as the "exciter", mounted on another bracket behind the chimney and driven by a belt coupled to the main generator.

Showman's Locomotive had dimensions much the same as the above, but without the exciter dynamo and the crane.

Contractor's Locomotive again had dimensions the same but without the exciter, crane, main dynamo and dynamo platform, and with only a three-quarter length cab (the canopy finishing at the rear of the chimney). Others were fitted with a half cab (finishing half-way between the flywheel and chimney). Usually these locomotives were fitted with wider section hind wheels than the other classes.

Except for the Scenic type which was never built under 8nhp, the showman's and contractors' locomotives ranged in power from 5 to 8nhp. A few were built to special order up to 10nhp and above. Regarding the term "nominal horse power"; it in no way remotely resembled the comparison of work capacity to that of the horse, but merely denoted a size of engine. It is interesting to note that although William Foster & Co frequently used the term "nhp", they often quoted their locomotives in "brake horse power", ie 65bhp (approximately 10nhp).

All other road locomotives were, with rare exceptions, of the double-crank type. They were spring mounted on both rear and front axles. All were fitted with differential locking gear, roping drum with 75 yards of wire rope, high- and low-pressure injectors, boiler-feed water pump fitted mostly by special order, three-speed gears, flywheel brake, hind-wheel rim brakes, steam water lifter, Pickering governors, tender and belly tanks with total capacity for 5/8nhp 230 gallons, Scenic type 350gal. Haulage power for 5nhp was 25 tons, for Scenic, 40 tons. Weight in working order: 5nhp, 12 tons; Scenic, 15 tons. They were legally entitled to haul a train of three trucks or wagons and a two-wheeled water-cart at a speed of 4mph, reduced to 2mph through towns.

Now that the days of the road locomotive have unhappily passed it is safe for me to say that when out of sight of an officer of the law, it was quite capable of doing 8 to 12mph with ease. In the days when these engines were used for furniture removals I have, on more than one occasion, driven a Burrell 8hp road loco with three pantechnicons behind it at speeds of this nature quite unconcernedly, except at the sight of a policeman.

It was indeed a beautiful sight to see a locomotive and its train trundling through the countryside. What excitement in those far off days to see two, three, or even four Showman's engines hauling the "Fair" to your town or village. Although I drove a heavy locomotive for a living during the day, when the fair came to our village I would be there—not on the rides, but talking to the drivers. Fascinated by the gentle rocking to and fro of the engines, I would listen to the faint click of a belt fastener as it passed over the dynamo pulley, the whining of the dynamo ever changing as the load varied, and always there would be the intoxicating smell of hot oil and steam in the air on a warm and still summer night. Those who have never experienced this feeling have never been to a fair.

What better example of harnessed power under a master's control than such as the firm of Norman E. Box Ltd, now alas no more, with three of their huge locomotives coupled to a load of 75 tons or more, each driver in perfect synchronisation of movement with the other. Such a sight as this will never again be seen, more is the pity.

Gone too are the road locomotives of Pickfords and many others too numerous to name. Perhaps their epitaph should read: "We were killed by the craving for speed, and to make room for oil."

Before leaving the subject of the Showman's engine, I have a vivid recollection of a secondhand Burrell 5hp 3-speed loco being brought to our yard at home for the owner of a travelling "Moving Picture Show". It was to be completely overhauled and fitted with a platform to the smokebox, and a dynamo with an output of 110 volts and 100 amperes. This was to supply the power for the one projector, three arc-lights and many small lamps at the façade and pay-box, three arclights on slings in the auditorium and numerous small lamps.

When the repairs and alterations had been completed the proprietor required one of our own drivers to go with the outfit to instruct his son in the arts of driving a steam engine. Being inspired by the glitter of a showman's life I volunteered for the job, and to my utter amazement was granted permission by my brother, our general manager, to go, but for four days only.

A trial run took place in our yard with the old silent films of

Burrell Showman's Road Loco No 2894 *"Centaur"*
(ex. Lord Fisher). Registration No FK 1463. Built 1907.
8nhp. Photographed at White Waltham Steam Fair.

Charlie Chaplin and others, at that time all the rage, being shown with great success. That night the tent was taken down and packed, and the next day saw us in a small town some fifteen or so miles away. The first show, an hour in length, went smoothly enough, then came the moment to strike the arc in the projector for the second show. Something—I never knew what—must have been a little out of order, for at that second there was a blinding flash and all lights went out, including those on the engine. The piano suddenly stopped playing the introduction. Then with screams and shouts mixed with exceedingly bad language, dozens of bodies came from under the skirt of the tent into the open air, some running for home, some to the nearest pub, while others gathered round the harassed proprietor

(*Left*) Burrell Showman's Engine No 3443 "*Lord Nelson*". Registration No CO 3822. Built 1913. 8nhp. DCC.
(*Bottom left*) Burrell Showman's Engine No 3884 "*Gladiator*". Registration No X·H 5728. Built 1921. 8nhp. DCC.
(*Below*) Burrell Showman's Engine No 3159 "*The Gladiator*". Registration No CO 3823. Built 1909. 7nhp. DCC.

Opposite
(*Top left*) Burrell Showman's Engine No 3949 "*Princess Mary*". Registration No NO 8287. Built 1923. 8nhp. DCC.
(*Top right*) Burrell Showman's Engine No 3847 "*Princess Marina*". Registration No CL 4483. Built 1920. 6nhp.
(*Right*) Burrell Showman's Engine No 3933 "*Princess Mary*". Registration No FJ 2041. Built 1922. 7nhp. DCC.

demanding their money back. This then was my first taste of the life of a showman.

In the cold light of dawn the next morning the fault was traced and repaired, but instead of showing in the same town that night it was deemed expedient to move on to another twenty miles away. I have a feeling that our fame reached that village long before us, judging by the hostility shown by the local inhabitants. However, the showmanship of Jack Collins the proprietor easily won the day. The piano was carried to the staging at the entrance by the pay-box. Then after ten minutes of lively songs and marshal music he announced that the first show of the evening would be free. That tent was full to bursting in minutes.

I was so enthralled by show life that it came as a great shock when, a week after I had left home, I was abruptly escorted back there by an irate brother. So ended the career of a budding young showman.

Opposite
Burrell Road Loco No 3202 *"Bampton Castle"*. Registration
No TA 1973. Built 1910. 6nhp. DCC. 3 speed.

Burrell Showman's Engine No 3912 *"Dragon"*.
Registration No CO 4485. Built 1922. 8nhp. DCC.

Opposite
Fowler Showman's Engine No 15653 "*Renown*".
Registration No CU 978. Built 1920. 7nhp. Class R3.
DCC. Before and after restoration.

Fowler Showman's Engine No 20223 "*Supreme*"
Registration No EV 5313. Built 1934. 10nhp. DCC. Class B6.

Steam Yachts. Photographed at Wadsworth.

(*Above*) Marenghi 98 Key Organ. Built 1911.
(*Top*) Mortier 101 Key Organ.

(*Above*) Three abreast Gallopers.
(*Top*) Gavioli 89 Key Organ.

Fowler Road Loco No 14754 "*Endeavour*". Registration
No NO 459. Built 1920. 7nhp. 13 tons. DCC. Class A9.

Opposite
Fowler Road Loco No 9456 "*Jess*". Registration No
KK 3634. Built 1902. DCC. Class A4.

(*Right*) Fowler Road Loco No 15371 "*General Smuts*". Registration No FJ 1526. Built 1919. 7nhp. Type A9.
(*Below*) Fowler Showman's Engine No 15652 "*Repulse*". Registration No CU 977. Built 1920. 7nhp. Class R3. Prior to restoration. Photographed at Billingshurst.

Burrell Road Loco No 2646. Registration No AD 8923. Built 1904. 7nhp. SCC. Before and after restoration.

McLaren Road Loco No 1652 "*Boadicea*". Registration
No WF 1864. Built 1919. 10nhp. 14 tons.

5 *Motor Tractors or Light Locomotives*

Looking back over the years there is no doubt that the steam tractor left its mark in the history of road haulage, its pinnacle of fame being in the 1920s. Strictly speaking the tractor was virtually a light road locomotive built to comply with the Heavy Motor Car Order of 1904 to a weight limit of 5 tons. Legally it was allowed to haul one trailer only, at a speed of 5 mph.

The Heavy Motor Car Order, I have been led to believe, though I cannot vouch for the truth of this, was instigated by the various county councils, who continued to raise hell, rightly or wrongly, about the amount of damage being done to the roads by the heavy locomotive. With the coming of the tarred road surface this may have had a ring of truth about it, but in my own opinion and that of one or two rural district and county surveyors of a bygone age, the road loco actually made our main roads by consolidating the foundations. To convince the councillors and the clerk to the county of this was, however, quite another matter.

When solid rubber tyres came into being and were fitted to the wheels, the heavy locomotive was given a reprieve and was able to hold its own for a few more years. The showman's loco, in particular, benefited in this way. I believe the owner actually got a reduction in his road fund tax, strange as it may seem.

Steam tractors were built mainly in the 5-ton category by the various makers, but W. Tasker & Sons of Andover achieved quite a name by the production of a 3-ton as well as a 5-ton version. One 3-tonner in particular became quite famous after it had been purchased by a lady, a great animal lover, who paid for it to be kept in steam at the bottom of a notoriously steep hill to render assistance to the heavily laden dray horses who passed that

way. This wonderful little tractor, now beautifully preserved, is with us still proudly bearing the letters "R.S.P.C.A." upon the side motion plates.

Wallis & Steevens, of Basingstoke, also made a 3-ton steam tractor, an exceedingly good one too. It was a common sight before World War I to see these little engines coupled to a light trailer or van delivering animal feeding stuffs to farmers. Occasionally, too, you might even see one coupled to a small pantechnicon busily engaged in the business of a short-haul furniture removal. Manufacturers other than Tasker and Wallis may have made a 3-ton engine, but of these I have no personal knowledge.

The 5-ton tractor built by Wallis & Steevens—I refer now to the "oil bath" type—was a masterpiece in economy. The only grudge I personally had against it was that the driver needed to be a contortionist and possess four pairs of hands to enable him to pack the piston and slide valve glands. On second thoughts it may have been that I was too big and clumsy to work in the narrow space between the cylinders and the oil bath.

Every manufacturer of traction engines, I believe without exception, produced a tractor of some kind between the years 1900 and 1925. Some were exceptionally good, some just average, and of others the least said of them the better. For my money there was nothing ever built that could outshine the Burrell 5-ton "Gold Medal Tractor". But don't let this statement fool you, for it is well known in the steam world of today, and of yesterday too for that matter, that I am heavily biased toward any engine manufactured by Charles Burrell, except perhaps his double chain drive steam wagon, but more of that later. His "Gold Medal", I am convinced, was the most powerful and fastest 3-speed tractor ever seen on the road in the early years. I have a vivid recollection of a journey made on one of these engines with a pantechnicon coupled behind, when, with my brother Cyril at the regulator, we covered 19 miles in two hours, including one stop for water.

My next choice would be the Tasker 5-ton chain-drive "Little Giant" tractor. It was very powerful and beautifully sprung on the rear axle with "Hoar's Patent Equalizing Spring Balancing Arrangement", to give its full title. But, Oh! The maintenance problems concerning it.

Another great feature of the Tasker tractor was the row of four 3in smoke tubes at the top of the boiler, a definite advantage in the matter of easy steaming. One characteristic of this tractor disliked by so many in the maintenance department, including myself, was the high- and low-pressure slide valves set obliquely in the steam-chest, something after the pattern used by Fowler's. In the absence of the correct machine for the job it thus became necessary to do it the hard way—with a block-file and a flat scraper, a veritable arm- back- and heart-aching killer.

Fowler, Aveling & Porter, Garrett, Clayton & Shuttleworth, Foster, Marshall and Ransomes, Sims & Jefferies were but a few of the most well known of the tractor manufacturers from 1904 onwards. In the late 1920s other famous names appeared, among them the Mann Steam Cart Co, Robey, with its patent round firebox needing no crown or side stays, Sentinel, with its vertical boiler and underslung engine, and lastly Foden, with the famous "D" type tractor.

The tractor was also a firm favourite among the showground people. Many were to be seen in the 1920s complete with dynamo and platform, twisted brass on the cab standards and stays, with brass stars and other emblems placed at points where they could be seen to the best advantage. It is indeed fortunate for all steam lovers, enthusiasts and old timers like myself, that specimens of most of the makes of tractor are still with us, beautifully preserved by their proud possessors and painted mostly in the original livery of the first owner.

Between the years 1904 and 1919 tractors were on iron-shod wheels, but unlike the traction engine the strakes were of wider material and set closer together with an approximate $\frac{3}{4}$in gap between each one. In the '20s, tractors were beginning to appear with wheels specially prepared to take a press-on solid rubber tyre. Perhaps I should explain this more fully; a press-on tyre comprised a 3in layer of solid rubber vulcanised to a thick endless band of steel. The whole tyre was placed under a huge hydraulic press and squeezed over the rim of the engine wheel at a pressure of from 15 to 20 tons per square inch. This same process was also used on the wheels of the last road locomotives that were built.

The introduction of the rubber tyre to tractors and locomotives effected a great economy in running costs and repair bills, as well as providing a greater road adhesion.

(*Above*) Aveling & Porter Tractor No 9170 "*Shamrock*".
Registration No KN 9352. Built 1920. 5 tons. Class KND.
(*Top right*) Aveling & Porter Tractor No 9225.
Registration No CJ 4160. Built 1920. Photographed at
Bishop's Castle 1970.
(*Right*) Aveling & Porter Tractor No 11997 "*Lucy May*".
Registration No KO 6739. Built 1928. 5nhp. 7¼ tons.
Comp.S/V.

(*Above*) Burrell Tractor No 3894 "*Saint Brannock*".
Registration No NX 947. Built 1921. 6nhp.
(*Top*) Burrell Tractor No 3689 "*Sunrise*". Registration
No BP5927. Built 1915. 4nhp. 5 tons.

(*Above*) Burrell Tractor No 4072 "*Tinkerbelle*".
Registration No PH 2900. Built 1927. 5 tons. Comp.
(*Top*) Burrell Tractor No 3718 "*Lion*". Registration
No AH 297. Built 1916. 5 tons.

(*Above*) Burrell Tractor No 3433 "*Peter Pan*".
Registration No AH 0108. Built 1912. 5 tons.
Photographed at Church Stretton 1967.
(*Left*) Burrell Tractor No 3631 "*Kathleen*".
Registration No OR 2729. Built 1915. 5 tons.

Opposite
Burrell Tractor No 3618 "*Princess Royal*".
Registration No TD 4276. Built 1914. 4nhp. 5 tons.

Opposite
Clayton & Shuttleworth Tractor No 49008.
Registration No VJ 5861. Built 1926. 5 tons.

Fowler Tractor No 14412. Registration No U 4662.
Built 1918. 4nhp. Class T3.

(*Above*) Garrett Tractor No 33219
"*Vindictive*". Registration No BJ 6180.
Built 1918. 4nhp. 5 tons. DCC.
(*Left*) Garrett Tractor No 34789 "*Queenie*".
Registration No YB 7841. Built 1926.

(*Above*) Garrett Tractor No 33738 "*Lord Raglan*". Registration No BJ 4791. Built 1919. 4nhp. 5 tons.
(*Left*) Garrett Tractor No 33829 "*Empress*". Registration No BJ 5157. Built 1920. 5 tons.

(*Left*) Tasker Tractor No 1822. Registration No HO 2930. Built 1920. 5 tons. Type B2.

(*Right*) Robey Tractor No 37657 "*The Guv'nor*". Registration No AP 9341. Built 1918. 4nhp. 5 tons. Photographed at Appleford 1970.
(*Bottom right*) Robey Tractor No 41492. Registration No FE 5736. Built 1923.

Opposite
Garrett Tractor No 33991 "*Patricia*". Registration No FX 1300. Built 1921.

Mann Tractor No 1425 "*Little Jim*". Registration No
U 7075. Built 1920. 4 tons.

6 *Road Rollers*

As Charles Burrell, John Fowler and William Foster held pride of place in the realms of the road locomotive, so Aveling & Porter, of Rochester, made themselves famous with the production of their road roller. The symbol of the rampant horse mounted on the front of all their products became known throughout the world. It has been said that an Aveling roller could be found in practically every country in which a Briton had set foot, and this I can well believe.

Very early in the 1850s, Thomas Aveling began making his steam rollers. Crude as these engines may appear to us today they certainly found favour with the county councils and contractors in those far-off days. So true was this that by 1900 the name of Aveling & Porter had reached the end of the earth. According to an old chap I once knew many years ago, a real Aveling fan, he cherished the idea that they might be using a few Aveling's in loftier regions! He had driven traction engines and rollers for more than 60 years, and was over 85 years of age when he asked me the following question.

"AAh, 'snow. Thee's a hedicated man, Zur. Can'st tell I if tez likely as they'd 'ave ingins up thur?" began old Tam Palmer, seriously, pointing the stem of his pipe in the direction of the sky.

"I don't know, Tam," I replied. "I've never heard of any in use up there. I expect transporting them is the main problem."

"AAh," drawled Tam, with a touch of disappointment in his voice and dragging hard at his pipe, "You'm settled 'en fer I. I ben' gwain thar now; I be gwain down along."

Aveling's, I feel sure, patented more fittings for, and varieties of, rollers than any other manufacturer. They made them from 3 to 20 tons in weight, with various kinds of scarifiers fitted for tearing up the roads before levelling. In some the top motion of the roller was fitted with the common "D" type slide valve, others with the piston valve. All sizes were available fitted with the standard firebox for burning high-grade coal, or the large firebox for service abroad to burn wood or inferior coal—the "colonial" type. There were single-cylinder and compound designs. The variety seemed endless.

A special type was produced for rolling hot tarmacadam. This was known as the Quick Reversing "Tandem" roller. It was fitted with a vertical boiler, and a horizontal double-cylinder engine which could be reversed without shutting off the steam, thus cutting to a minimum the time the roller would be stationary on the hot tarmac, and rendering less likely the leaving of an impression by the rolls which would be extremely difficult to erase. This roller was also fitted with steam steerage, a small quick-acting 3-cylinder engine, controlled by a hand lever operating a worm and quandrant connected to the front roll fork. An account of the hazards of driving one of these machines is given in a book entitled *I Worked with Traction Engines*.

Although Aveling & Porter manufactured many traction engines, steam wagons, a few road locomotives and sets of steam-ploughing tackle, I feel it could be correct to say that the number of rollers built by them would exceed the total production of rollers of all the other firms put together. I have no proof of this, of course; it is my own assumption, induced perhaps by the knowledge of one firm of contractors alone purchasing 200 rollers in a very short space of time.

Every known manufacturer of traction engines in this country built his version of what he considered a steam roller should be, and tried his best to outdo his rivals. Some not even in traction-engine production, like Greens for example, built quite a number. A few almost reached a par with Aveling's, while others failed completely, not because they could not build a perfectly good roller, but, in my own opinion, because they were unable to dislodge Aveling's from the market they had found.

In the last days of steam one or two firms amalgamated, believing in the adage "United we stand . . ." But they were subsequently lost never to return, to our lasting regret. Despite those bad years Aveling & Porter, together with our old friends Wallis & Steevens of Basingstoke with their "Advance" roller, survived to continue building them until what might be known as "Oil Politics" overtook them. The name of Aveling & Porter changed to Aveling-Barford, and steam changed to diesel. It is generally thought that the last Aveling steam roller built by Aveling-Barford for use in this country was completed in February 1948, maker's No AH162. This roller is now preserved at Camborne, Cornwall.

Opposite
Aveling & Porter Roller No 10350. Registration No KX 6838. Built 1922. Photographed in children's playground—Slough 1970.

(*Above*) Aveling & Porter Roller No 3430
"*Sarah*". Registration No PB 9801. Built
1894. $10\frac{1}{2}$ tons.
(*Right*) Aveling & Porter No 8752.
Registration No TA 2662. 8 tons. Taken at
Sellindge 1970.

(*Above*) Aveling & Porter Roller No 14150.
Registration No DW 7867. 8 tons. Photographed at
Northleach.
(*Top right*) Aveling & Porter Roller No 8837.
Registration No NO 1221. Built 1918. 12 tons.
(*Right*) Aveling & Porter Roller No 14062 "*Amy*"
Registration No HV 861. Built 1930. 10 tons.

(*Right*) Aveling & Porter Roller No 2941. Registration
No AL 9463. Built 1892. 10 tons.
(*Below*) Aveling & Porter Roller No 10190 "*Joy*"
Registration No FX 8654. Built 1922. 8 tons.

Opposite
Fowler Roller No 17950. Registration No CYY 424.
Built 1931. 8 tons. Class T3B, and
Fowler Roller No 15970. Registration No NW 6092.
Built 1924. 8 tons. Class T3.

Opposite
Burrell Roller No 3956 "*Pride of the Road*".
Registration No HT 8219. 11½ tons.

(*Above*) Burrell Roller No 3985. Registration No RK 2907.
8 tons.
(*Top right*) Burrell Roller No 4058. Registration No
PX 5192. Built 1926. 8 tons.
(*Right*) Burrell Roller No 4070 "*Charlie*". Registration
No WW 2181. Built 1927. 10 tons.

(*Above*) Fowler Roller No 18503.
Registration No GO 5298. Built 1931.
10 tons. Class DNB.
(*Left*) Fowler Roller No 16665.
Registration No DM 3918.

Opposite
Fowler Roller No.14674 "*Busy Bee*".
Registration No BW 9937. Built 1922.
10 tons. Class DH.

(*Right*) Ruston Proctor Roller No 48359
"*Pride of Barum*". Registration No TA 2894.
Built 1913. 11 tons.
(*Below*) Marshall Roller No 76963.
Registration No YA 8855. Built 1924.

(*Above*) Wallis & Steevens Roller No 2656
"*Little Tacker*". Registration No HO 5834.
Built 1921. 3 tons. Single cylinder.
(*Left*) Wallis & Steevens Simplicity Roller
No 7832. Built 1926. 3 tons.

Robey Tri-tandem No 45655 "*Herts Wanderer*".
Registration No VL 2773. Built 1930.

7 Steam Wagons

The man who first conceived the idea of making a steam wagon really started something. By the year 1860 there appeared to be more people having a "bash" at it than there were days in the year. I have been reading an account in a local Sussex paper dated April 1862 of a steam vehicle running about the streets of Horsham, presumably on a visit to the town. It was indeed enlightening to read: "... and as far as we could discern, the man at the helm had no difficulty in steering it in any direction he might think proper. The carriage was manufactured by Mr T. W. Cowan, Kent Iron Works, Greenwich. Its appearance is neat and compact, and it is constructed to carry twelve passengers comfortably. . . ." What a wonderful contraption that must have been!

It would take a very large book indeed simply to list the names of all those who tried to produce a really workable proposition, but somehow most of them just missed the mark. There were one or two in the early pioneering days who stood on the threshold of success, yet at the last minute turned away and focused their attention on what was then known as the "new fangled internal combustion engine" (more is the pity). They were of course Leyland, Stewart-Thornycroft and Clarkson. The first two mentioned gave up the chase very early on, and Clarkson I believe turned his attention to steam buses. As a young lad I remember these running in London. I recall too seeing one or two Clarkson lorries working in the Godalming area at about the same period (1910).

My first witnessing of a fatal accident involved a Clarkson lorry. As I remember it, it was an ungainly looking affair with a vertical boiler of the water tube type, something like the Merry-weather, with the engine just to the rear of it. In front was what looked like a radiator, but which was in fact a condenser. My father had taken me to Guildford for the day, and we were then making our way to the railway station to return home. As we turned from the bottom of the Portsmouth Road hill towards the station we were startled to hear the shrilling of a steam whistle, mingled with wild shouting. We looked to our left and saw the Clarkson careering down the hill apparently out of control. At the junction of four roads at the foot of the hill stood a patrolman in Automobile Association uniform with his back to the on-coming Clarkson, directing the traffic, unaware of his imminent danger. He turned at the last second, but too late. I saw him fall, but nothing else; my father's coat was thrown over my face ...

By 1910 many manufacturers such as Foden, Alchin, Atkinson, Clayton, Tasker, Aveling, Garrett, Yorkshire and Mann, although still on iron-shod wheels, were producing steam wagons that were economical, powerful and very reliable, making delivery agents and contractors really sit up and take notice. Then came the 1914 war. Like every other war it stirred up the inventiveness in man, and many improvements and modifications demanded by the War Department became possible through the metallurgists' evolvement of new metals, steels and alloys. The driving chain was one piece of equipment that was vastly improved. The new method of casting piston ring pots, from which the rings were turned, was another. A great boon was the re-modelling of the high-pressure injector, and the further development of the White's injector into the finest piece of steam equipment ever made. This type of injector was fitted to practically every make of steam wagon, and is still available today unaltered in design from 1916. Provided that the water in the engine's tank is cold I have known this injector work at from 10lb up to 230lb/sq in.

Later developments in the steam wagon brought much higher working pressures, the three-speed gears and greater efficiency, with the resultant economy in fuel. Some manufacturers stuck to the over-type wagon with locomotive pattern boilers, together with the chain transmission to the back axle, right up to 1930. Others like the Sentinel wagon, known as the under type, used a vertical boiler, with the engine mounted in the chassis under the body. In the later years Sentinel's changed from chain transmission to shaft drive.

Garrett's, of Leiston built an over-type wagon with a steam superheater, but it was not altogether successful. Later they too turned to the under type with much better fortune. Foden's in their latest design of the 1930s built two under types known as the "Speed 6" and the "Speed 12" with wonderful results. They were reputed to have claimed that their "Speed 12" was guaranteed to carry a load of 20 tons at a speed of 40mph. If this was factual in 1932, one wonders what might have happened regarding road transport had not the Road and Rail Traffic Act of 1930 intervened. Of one thing I am sure; we would not be breathing diesel and petrol fumes as we are today. Sometimes I feel in these old bones of mine that some day steam will return to our roads, but not in the form we knew of yesteryear. Think of what is happening in America with the steam car at the present time, and think long and well of the experiments carried out with the Sentinel-Dobel steam truck before you say "NEVER".

But back to steam wagons and boilers of the past. The Yorkshire Wagon Co Ltd departed widely from the normal basic pattern by fitting a revolutionary part-vertical and part-horizontal boiler across the front of the wagon and a vertical engine mounted behind it. This proved to be a very efficient wagon indeed, and was widely used all over the country with outstanding results in performance and economy.

You often look back upon the days of driving a steam wagon with a certain amount of nostalgia, and are rather apt to forget the hard work attached to it. When carting sand or stones in a non-tipping body, for example, every ounce of it had to be thrown up from the ground into the wagon by your fireman and yourself with shovels; you then drove like the clappers of hell to your destination and shovelled it all out again.

I have recollections of doing this kind of hard graft while carting sand used in foundry work. It was quarried near the Devil's Punch Bowl at Hindhead and our firm had contracted to transport it from the pit to Milford Station, for which the driver and his fireman would receive one shilling above their wages for every load they handled.

For a while we had two wagons on this job, one of our own, and one on hire to us. To speed things up we would throw the engines out of gear after passing the Punch Bowl, and coast like the wind practically the whole seven miles into Milford. This went on merrily until the day came when Bill Martin, the driver of the second wagon, while freewheeling blithely down the hill as usual, had occasion to avoid a horse and cart going in the same direction. Unable to pull up, he chose the ditch on the side of the road with disastrous results to the band brake on the back axle, which fouled a milestone on the verge. When at last everything came to a halt, Bill viewed the extent of the damage. Then to avoid being given the sack, he promptly put the engine back in gear and swore that the broken brake was the cause of the accident.

"Ah," exclaimed Bill to me later, "'ten't no good if yer don't git more artful, is it?"

Another sight that will never again be seen was the Alchin steam wagon belonging to the organist who toured the theatres all over the country. The "Grand Organ" would be erected on the stage, the Alchin supplying the 110 volts required to operate it. I well remember this steam wagon standing outside the Theatre Royal, North Street, Guildford, on one occasion in 1914. It was a lovely sight indeed with its twisted brass cab standards, its dynamo and platform fixed on the smokebox, the usual showman's decorations, and the brilliant paintwork of the box-body.

What a pity it all had to end. . . .

Foden D-type Tractor No 12370. Registration No TT 8659.
Built 1926.

Foden Wagon No 11892 *"Star of Acrise"*. Registration No
VKE 666H. Built 1927. Photographed at Acrise 1970.

Opposite
(*Top left*) Foden Wagon No 13008
"Little Alice". Registration No UR 1328.
Photographed at Biggin Hill Air Fair 1970.
(*Top right*) Foden D-type Tractor No 13784.
Registration No UX 9728. Built 1931.
(*Bottom left*) Mr. J. Hampshire
photographed with his Foden Wagon
No 13716 *"Peg O' My Heart"*.
Registration No RP 9208. Built 1930.
6 ton 3-way tipper.
(*Bottom right*) Foden D-type Tractor
No 13484 *"Talisman"*. Registration No
LG 8784. Built 1929.

Opposite
Super Sentinel Steam Wagon No 8109 *"The Chiltern Hundreds"*. Registration No YC 7914. Built 1929. Photographed at Redhill 1970.

(*Above*) Sentinel Steam Wagon No 9277. Registration No DKN 689. Built 1937. Type S4.
(*Top left*) Sentinel Steam Wagon No 8571. Registration No KF 6482. Built 1931. Class DG4.
(*Left*) Sentinel Steam Wagon No 9163. Registration No AER 800. Built 1935. Type S4.
Photographed at Appleford 1970.

(*Left*) Sentinel Steam Wagon No 8928. Registration No UJT 333. Built 1934. Type S6.

(*Right*) Sentinel Steam Wagon No 8992 "*Prince*". Registration No TJ 4148. Built 1934. Type S4.
(*Bottom right*) Super Sentinel No 5104. Registration No CA 6395. Built 1923.

Opposite
Sentinel No 5558. Registration No PD 1854. Built 1924.

Super Sentinel No 8393 *"HMS Sultan"*.
Registration No DX 9048. Built 1930. Photographed
at Beaulieu 1960 (*Above*) and at Liphook 1970 (*Left*).

(*Above*) Sentinel Timber Tractor No 8777 "*Old Bill*".
Registration No JB 1655. Built 1933. Class DG.
(*Left*) Sentinel Timber Tractor No 8756 "*Brutus*".
Registration No VN 4294. Built 1933. Class DG.

Sentinel Steam Wagon No 6979. Registration No YH 5763. Built 1927, and McLaren Agricultural Traction Engine No 547. Registration No BD 5448. Built 1896. 6nhp. Photographed at Redruth 1966.